FOREST
-feast-®

Inspiring Ingredients

By Kestrel Foods Ltd.

Contents

Introduction

Here at Forest Feast we dedicate much of our time to finding the finest dried fruit and nuts, from around the world, to add to our family of products. We strive to create the most vibrant of packaging and we lovingly produce our dried fruit and nuts to ensure they look their very best when we send them out into the world to find their way. As we believe that variety is the spice of life we sometimes coat our products in the finest Belgian Chocolate or roast them and add some exotic spices and flavours to give them a real point of difference.

One day, in a flash of inspiration, we realised that maybe our famously good Forest Feast dried fruit & nuts should be enjoyed in other ways. We shouldn't limit their potential before they start their journey in life and they should be encouraged to be adventurous and to try new experiences and flavours.

They are not just dried fruit and nuts for snacking but Inspiring Ingredients to be added to the finest of recipes and enjoyed by the entire family, at any time of the day. There is no occasion too great for Forest Feast and our dried fruit and nuts want to be there with you, in your kitchen, inspiring fantastic food, made from the freshest of ingredients.

We have put together some of our ideas on how to give our Forest Feast range a more adventurous journey in life. We hope you grasp this opportunity with both hands and go forwards with a fresh perspective of Forest Feast as one of life's Inspiring Ingredients.

Enjoy!
All at Forest Feast

Wonder Fruit Bars are easy to make and crammed full of Forest Feast fruity goodness. Perfect as a mid afternoon 'pick me up' or an after school snack!

Wonder Fruit Bars

Makes 18
Preheat oven to 150°C/300°F/gas mark 2.

Ingredients:

200g unsalted butter
50g golden syrup
1 tin of condensed milk (397g)
1 teaspoon of vanilla extract
300g fine porridge oats
175g Forest Feast Wonder Berries (includes dried cranberries, goji berries, blackcurrants, physalis, blueberries and strawberries.)
30g Forest Feast Sunflower Seeds
30g Forest Feast Toasted Pumpkin Seeds
160g Forest Feast Malatya Apricots, chopped

Method:

- Line a 9 inch baking tin with baking parchment.
- Weigh all the dry ingredients into a large mixing bowl (porridge oats, Wonder Berries, seeds, chopped apricots) and thoroughly mix together.
- Use a saucepan to gently heat the butter and golden syrup along with the condensed milk.
- When it is just melted and no more, quickly add the vanilla and pour over the dry ingredients, mix until well coated.
- Pour the mixture into the prepared baking tin and bake for 45 minutes until golden brown.
- Remove from the oven and when cool, place in the fridge until firm.
- Cut into 18 little bars (6 across x 3 down) and store in an airtight container.

Perfect as an after school snack!

Blueberry Breakfast Buns are ideal for life 'on the go', to ensure that a speedy start does not mean missing out on the most important meal of the day. They're wee buns to make and you can freeze them so there's no excuse!

Blueberry Breakfast Buns

Makes 9 large buns
Preheat oven to 175°C/350°F/gas mark 3.

Ingredients:

200g plain flour
1 teaspoon of baking powder
¼ teaspoon of baking soda
A tiny pinch of salt
200g low fat cream cheese, softened
100g butter, softened
150g light brown sugar
2 large eggs, at room temperature
40mls milk
5 drops of vanilla extract
80g Forest Feast Unbelievable Blueberries
50g blueberry jam
To decorate: A small handful of Forest Feast Pumpkin Seeds and fresh blueberries. A little icing to drizzle

Method:

- Use an electric mixer to beat together the cream cheese, butter and sugar until smooth, this will take about 3 minutes.
- Sift the flour, baking powder, baking soda and salt together removing any lumps.
- Lightly whisk the eggs, milk and vanilla together.
- Turn the mixer down to the lowest setting and gradually add the liquid and dry mixes alternately until smooth and creamy, finish by stirring in the dried blueberries.
- Spoon the batter into each muffin case to about three quarters full.
- Drop a teaspoon of blueberry jam onto the top of each bun and swirl using the tip of a sharp knife.
- Bake for 25-30 minutes, or until a skewer inserted in the centre of the bun comes out clean.
- Decorate with blueberries, pumpkin seeds and a drizzle of icing.

for life 'on the go'

Pour the dressing over the salad and
serve with warm crusty bread.

At Forest Feast we love our fantastic exotic Carabao Mango from the sun drenched isles of the Philippines. When you can resist the temptation just to enjoy it as it is, our signature Prawn, Mango & Pomegranate Salad is simply fresh and delicious.

Prawn, Mango and Pomegranate Salad

Serves 4

Ingredients:

400g cooked & peeled prawns
1 small red onion
1 bag of mixed salad leaves
200g Forest Feast Exotic Dried Mango
50g Forest Feast Perfect Pomegranate
½ mild chilli
A handful of fresh mint
A handful of coriander leaves

Dressing:
3 tablespoons of virgin olive oil
1 tablespoon of lime juice
1 teaspoon of honey

The key ingredient

Perfect pomegranate.

Method:

- Thinly slice the red onion, the dried Mango and the chilli.
- Place in a large salad bowl along with the rest of the ingredients.
- Make the dressing by whisking the olive oil, lime juice and honey together.
- Pour the dressing over the salad and serve with warm crusty bread.

Whisk olive oil, lime juice and honey togethes

Spicy Chicken and Fruit Wrap

Serves 2

Ingredients:

1 large cooked chicken breast
A few Forest Feast Jumbo Agen Prunes
A handful of sultanas
A pinch of curry powder
A spoonful of low fat mayonnaise
2 tortilla wraps
Salad leaves
Chopped spring onions

Method:

- Chop the chicken breast and Agen Prunes and place in a bowl.
- Add the sultanas, curry powder and mayonnaise and mix well.
- Lay the tortilla wraps on a chopping board and fill with salad leaves, chopped spring onions and top with the fruity chicken mixture.
- Roll up tightly and cut each wrap in half to serve.

Salad Days

Greek Feta, Watermelon and Pistachio Salad

Serves 4

Ingredients:

¼ Watermelon
160g Feta Cheese, cubed
A handful of Forest Feast California Pistachio Nuts, shelled
A handful of fresh mint, shredded

Method:

- Remove the skin of the watermelon and chop into bite size pieces.
- Mix with the Feta cheese, California pistachio nuts and mint to serve.

PEN • STAY FRESH • RE

Best Before
See back of p

FOREST
-feast-

Jumbo Agen

Prunes

to eat s

This Chicken and Coco Mango Curry is bursting with flavour and can be made in a flash. The chicken needs to be thinly sliced to poach quickly in the curry sauce, keeping it juicy and tender. If chicken isn't your thing, swap for some prawns or a vegetarian option of mushrooms, peppers and spinach which works really well. And don't forget to season with curry powder to taste.

Chicken and Mango Curry

Serves 4

Ingredients:

1 tablespoon of light oil
1 onion, finely sliced
1 tin of half fat coconut milk
400mls chicken stock
100g Forest Feast Coco Mango, finely chopped
2 garlic cloves, crushed
15g grated ginger
3 dessertspoons of tomato purée
2 dessertspoons of medium curry powder (depending on how hot you like it)
Juice of ½ a lime
3 large chicken fillets, sliced in half horizontally and then sliced quite thinly
4 spring onions, washed and chopped
7g fresh coriander leaves and stalks finely chopped

Method:

- Fry the onion in a little oil until soft, then add the coconut milk, chicken stock, Coco Mango and simmer for 5 minutes allowing the Coco Mango to dissolve.
- Add the garlic, ginger, tomato purée and curry powder as you turn up the heat and bring the sauce to boiling point. Reduce the heat immediately and simmer for 8 minutes until thick and creamy.
- Add the raw chicken and cook for a further 3 - 4 minutes.
- Finally stir in the spring onions, coriander and finish with a squeeze of lime.
- Serve with steamed Jasmine rice.

Pine Nuts give great flavour to this Mediterranean dish which is perfect for a long lazy lunch on a hazy summer's day.

Spaghetti with Chorizo, Spinach and Pine Nuts

Serves 4

Ingredients:

You will need enough spaghetti for four people, simply follow the packet cooking instructions and cook while you make the sauce.

For the sauce:
1 tablespoon of light olive oil
1 onion, finely chopped
50g chorizo sausage, cut in half lengthways and then chopped into small pieces
40g Forest Feast Pine Nuts
60g sun blush tomatoes, cut in half
1 clove of garlic, crushed
A small pinch of chilli flakes
400mls chicken stock
100g extra light cream cheese
100g baby spinach leaves
15g basil leaves, finely chopped
A little salt and pepper
25g grated fresh parmesan

To serve: Extra parmesan / Crusty bread

Method:

- Heat the olive oil in a large saucepan and fry the onion until very soft.
- Tip in the chorizo and cook for about 3 minutes. As it cooks it will release its delicious smokiness and will lend a pale yellow tinge to the onions. Add the pine nuts and allow them to toast in the oil.
- Quickly add the tomatoes, garlic and chilli flakes and stir in the chicken stock, bringing it to the boil. Reduce the temperature immediately and simmer for a few minutes before stirring in the cream cheese. Continue to simmer for a few more minutes until the sauce thickens slightly.
- Finish the sauce by adding basil, spinach, a little salt and a few twists of black pepper. Sprinkle in the grated parmesan and stir until the spinach wilts and the parmesan melts.
- By this time your spaghetti should be cooked perfectly, simply drain it and tip into the sauce, stirring to make sure the pasta is completely coated in the sauce.
- Serve immediately with a few extra shavings of parmesan and some warm crusty bread.

Pistachio and Herb Crusted Hake is the ideal serving suggestion for seafood fans as it works equally well with Haddock, Cod or Salmon. Try not to overcook the fish, as the flesh should be white, juicy and break away in large pieces. The dish can be prepared in advance, kept in the fridge and baked when required.

Pistachio and Herb Crusted Hake

Serves 4
Preheat oven to 180°C/350°F/gas mark 4.

Ingredients:

4 pieces of Hake fillet (about 180g each)
2 teaspoons of olive oil
40g fresh parmesan, grated

For the crust:
80g bread
1 shallot
1 clove of garlic
80g Forest Feast California Pistachios, shelled
7g basil
7g flat leaf parsley
A pinch of chilli powder
Salt and freshly ground pepper

Method:

- Place all the crust ingredients into a food processor and whiz for a few minutes until they resemble fine green breadcrumbs.
- Rub the hake pieces with a little olive oil and place onto a non-stick roasting tray before dividing the crust topping into four and pressing on top of the fish. Finish by sprinkling the parmesan on top and place into a hot oven for 15 minutes until the fish is cooked through and the crust is crunchy and slightly golden.
- Keep the fish warm until you are ready to serve.
- Serve with a summer salad of baby leaves, red onion and tomatoes, or for a hearty meal try creamy mash and vegetables.

Optional – Sauce:1 teaspoon of light oil, 2 spring onions (finely sliced), 2 rashers of smoked bacon, 150mls whipping cream, salt and pepper

- Fry off the spring onion and bacon in a little oil for 2 minutes, add the cream and bring to the boil, cook for a few minutes until the cream has thickened, season with salt and pepper.

With a few fresh and some staple larder ingredients you can prepare this broth in as little as 10 minutes. The sweetness from our Coco Mango works a treat with prawns, garlic and coriander, not forgetting the all important chilli kick - essential in Thai cuisine.

Thai Prawn and Noodle Broth

Serves 6 (very hungry people)

Ingredients:

1 tablespoon of light oil
1 large onion, very finely sliced
100g fresh Shitake mushrooms, cut in half and then finely sliced
1 red pepper, finely sliced
100g Forest Feast Coco Mango, roughly chopped
1½ litres of fish stock
400mls of reduced fat coconut milk (1 can)
2 cloves of garlic, crushed
½ a fresh red chilli, finely chopped
30g fresh ginger, grated
2 teaspoons of hot curry powder
180g dried egg noodles
100g spinach
400g cooked prawns
20g finely chopped fresh coriander leaves and stalks

Method:

- Heat a large saucepan and gently fry the onion in a little oil, when soft add the sliced Shitake mushrooms and red pepper- fry for 2 minutes.
- Quickly pour in the stock, coconut milk and Coco Mango pieces and allow this to come to the boil, then reduce the temperature and simmer gently while the Coco Mango dissolves.
- Stir in the garlic, chilli, ginger and curry powder. Allow this to simmer gently for another 3 minutes before adding your egg noodles.
- The egg noodles will only take about 3 or 4 minutes to cook in the broth, so just before they are ready, tip in the spinach and prawns. By the time the spinach has wilted and the prawns have warmed through the noodles will be perfectly cooked.
- Sprinkle with coriander, ladle into warm bowls, serve and enjoy.

The sweetness from our Coco Mango works a treat with prawns, garlic and coriander.

STAY FRESH

Best Before
See back

FOREST
feast

Carabao
Coco
Mango

An exotic mouth-watering combination
of Mango and Coconut

Fantastic Physalis, also known as Wild Cape Gooseberry, perfectly compliments and contrasts with our sweet Mouth-watering Mango and makes the most delicious sweet & sour salsa to enjoy with Lamb Burgers.

Lamb Burgers with Sweet & Sour Salsa

Makes 4

Ingredients:

For the lamb burgers:

500g lean minced lamb
½ small onion, finely chopped
1 garlic clove, crushed
1 small pinch of chilli flakes
1 level teaspoon of cinnamon
1 teaspoon of tomato purée
A small handful of fresh mint leaves, finely chopped
A small handful of fresh parsley leaves, finely chopped
1 egg, lightly beaten

For the salsa:

80g Forest Feast Mouth-watering Mango, finely sliced
80g Forest Feast Fantastic Physalis
1 shallot, finely sliced
½ mild red chilli, finely sliced
45g brown sugar
The juice of 2 limes
A small handful of mint leaves
A small handful of coriander leaves

To serve:

4 small crusty rolls, cut in half and lightly toasted, baby salad leaves

Method:

- Make the salsa first, so the fruit has time to absorb the lime juice and will be juicy and plump by the time your burgers are cooked. Tip the chopped Mango and Physalis into a bowl and mix with shallot, chilli, mint and coriander. Put the lime juice and sugar into a bowl and microwave on high for 30 seconds to dissolve the sugar, and then mix into the salsa.
- Combine the burger ingredients together and form into six large meatballs, flatten out slightly to make burgers.
- Grill under a medium heat for 6 - 8 minutes on each side until golden brown and thoroughly cooked.
- Arrange the burgers on the rolls with salad, top with the salsa and serve with a mixed salad.

Cranberry Pork Fillet with Red Cabbage

Preheat oven to 180°C/350°F/gas mark 4.
Serves 6-8 people

Ingredients:

2 large pork fillets (about 560g each)
8 slices of Parma ham

For the stuffing:
½ small onion, chopped
1 granny smith apple, cored & grated
2 cloves of garlic, crushed
80g Forest Feast Incredible Cranberries
260g good quality pork sausage meat
180g breadcrumbs
8g finely chopped parsley
1 medium egg
Salt and freshly ground pepper

For the red cabbage:
1 tablespoon of olive oil
1 red onion, cut in half and finely sliced
1 medium sized red cabbage, quartered, cored & shredded
80g Forest Feast Incredible Cranberries
40g soft brown sugar
70mls balsamic vinegar
250mls vegetable stock
Salt and freshly ground pepper

Method: To make the stuffing

- Tip all the stuffing ingredients into a large bowl and mix until totally combined.
- Set the pork onto a chopping board and slice it horizontally along the side but not the whole way through, you want the fillet to open out like a book. Cover with a piece of cling film and bat slightly with a rolling pin, this will help tenderize the fillet. Discard the cling film and spread half the stuffing over the pork, covering it completely.
- On another board, lay 4 slices of Parma ham side by side to create a rectangular shape. Set the pork and stuffing on top and then roll up like a Swiss roll.
- Repeat this process to stuff and roll the second pork fillet with the remaining ingredients.
- Line a large roasting tray with tin foil and place the pork fillets on top - do not cover the meat with foil (you want the Parma ham to be crisp) and place into a hot oven for 40 minutes. Remove from the oven, cover with foil at this point and rest for 10 minutes before carving.

While the pork is roasting – cook the red cabbage

- Gently heat the olive oil in a large heavy bottom saucepan and fry the red onion for 3 minutes, tip in the shredded red cabbage and continue to fry for another 3 minutes.
- Stir in the cranberries, sugar, balsamic vinegar and vegetable stock while bringing to the boil.
- When the liquid reaches boiling point reduce the temperature to simmering, pop the lid on and allow the cabbage to gently cook for 25 minutes.
- Serve the sliced pork and cabbage with creamy mashed potato and green beans.

For an incredible Sunday lunch or when entertaining large numbers, our Cranberry Pork Fillet can be prepared a day in advance and is best served with really creamy mash and some healthy greens.

For a truly Moroccan experience, prepare our Spiced Lamb and Agen Prune Tagine in an earthenware pot with a tight fitting lid as it allows you to start the cooking process on your hob and then slowly braise the lamb in a low oven to enrich the earthy flavours of spices, herbs, red wine, prunes and butternut squash.

Spiced Lamb and Agen Prune Tagine

Serves 6
Preheat oven to 150°C/300°F/gas mark 2.

Ingredients:

1 large onion, roughly chopped
670g Lamb (we used 4 small leg steaks cut into 1 inch pieces)
1 teaspoon of cinnamon
1 teaspoon of turmeric
½ teaspoon of ground cumin
2 cloves of garlic, crushed
300mls lamb stock (made from stock cubes or powder)
300mls red wine (we used merlot)
250g Forest Feast Jumbo Agen Prunes
1 small butternut squash, peeled, seeded and chopped into 1 inch pieces
Salt and pepper
A small pinch of chilli flakes
15g chopped fresh mint
20g chopped fresh coriander (leaves and stalks)
To serve: Cooked couscous (enough for 6 people), 50g Forest Feast Flaked Almonds, lightly toasted

Method:

- Allow the lamb pieces to marinade in the red wine while you gather and prepare the remaining ingredients, this will begin to tenderise the meat.
- In your earthenware pot, fry the chopped onion in a little olive oil over a medium heat until softened.
- Remove the lamb from the wine, add to the hot pan and seal. Set the red wine aside, you will need it soon.
- Add the cinnamon, turmeric, cumin and garlic to the meat and stir well to release the flavours.
- Quickly add the lamb stock, the red wine, Agen prunes, a good pinch of salt and a few grinds of pepper, stir as the liquid comes to the boil.
- Add the chopped squash and ¾ of the mint and coriander, now place the lid on and set the earthenware pot into a hot oven for 1½ hours.
- When the Tagine is ready, remove from the oven, stir in the remaining coriander and mint, then sprinkle with toasted chopped almonds. Serve piping hot with freshly cooked couscous.

We love the simple things in life and it really is amazing how a few natural ingredients can produce a salmon dish that is so inspired. We hope you'll love it too.

Maple and Cashew Glazed Salmon

Serves 4
Preheat oven to 200°C /400°F/gas mark 6.

Ingredients:

4 salmon fillets (about 180g each)
100g Forest Feast Natural Cashew Nuts, Chopped

For the marinade:
6 tablespoons of light soy sauce
4 tablespoons of maple syrup
The juice and zest of 1 lime
25g fresh ginger, grated
1 tablespoon of vegetable oil
2 cloves of garlic, finely chopped
1 pinch of chilli powder

To serve: 200g uncooked Basmati rice, 2 small heads of pak choi

Method:

- Put all ingredients for the marinade into a large mixing bowl and add the salmon. Leave to marinade for 30 minutes.
- Remove the salmon fillets from the marinade and set onto a non-stick roasting tray.
- Pour the remaining marinade into a frying pan and boil for 2 – 3 minutes until thick, then pour over the top of the salmon and bake in a hot oven for about 7 minutes. After 3 minutes sprinkle the chopped cashew nuts over the fish and return to the oven for the remaining 4 minutes.
- While the salmon is roasting stir fry the pak choi in a little oil and cook the basmati rice according to packet instructions.

Duck is perfectly complimented by our Scrumptious Sour Cherries as the slight acidity of the fruit cuts through the rich meat. We like to use healthier cooking techniques where possible and a top tip is to place the duck skin side down in a non-stick pan over a medium heat allowing it to cook for about 10 minutes – this process is called rendering, which gets rid of fat, therefore creating a crispy skin.

Spicy Duck with Sour Cherry Couscous

Serves 4
Preheat oven to 180°C/350°F/gas mark 4.

Ingredients for the duck:

4 Barbary duck breasts, skin on
(each weighing about 180g)
A little salt
1 teaspoon of Chinese five spice powder

For the dressing:

2 tablespoons of Chinese plum sauce
2 tablespoons of light olive oil
1 tablespoon of red wine vinegar
A small pinch of chilli flakes

For the couscous salad:

200g couscous
250mls chicken stock
1 tablespoon of olive oil
1 red onion, halved and finely sliced
1 clove of garlic, crushed
A pinch of chilli flakes
80g Forest Feast Scrumptious Sour Cherries
15g fresh coriander, finely chopped
15g fresh mint, finely chopped
100g wild rocket leaves

Method:

- Use a sharp knife to lightly score the skin of the duck breasts and then rub with salt.
- Heat a heavy-based pan over low heat. Add the duck breasts, skin-side down, and leave for about 10 minutes until the fat is nearly all extracted and the skin is golden brown and crisp.
- To finish cooking the duck breasts simply rub Chinese five spice powder over the flesh and skin of each duck breast, place on to a roasting tray and set into a hot oven to cook for about 4 minutes. The meat should feel slightly springy when pressed if you want it cooked to medium. Set on a plate and cover with tin foil to rest for 5 minutes.
- Tip the couscous into a bowl, boil the chicken stock and pour over, stir and allow to stand for 10 minutes while you prepare the rest of the salad.
- Gently heat the oil in a large frying pan and cook the onions until soft and golden, add the garlic, chilli and sour cherries and cook for a further 3 minutes before adding to the couscous along with the chopped coriander and mint.
- Whisk the dressing ingredients together.
- Slice the duck and serve with couscous salad sprinkled with rocket leaves and a little dressing.

For those who are really well organised, Pancetta wrapped Chicken can be prepared in advance and left in the fridge overnight. This allows the smoked pancetta flavours to mingle with the chicken and sweetness of our gorgeous Malatya Apricots and California Pistachios.

Pancetta wrapped Chicken with Apricot and Pistachio Stuffing

Serves 4
Preheat oven to 200°C /400°F/gas mark 6.

Ingredients:

4 chicken fillets
16 strips of smoked pancetta
1 tablespoon of olive oil
½ onion, finely chopped
100g fine breadcrumbs
80g Forest Feast Malatya Apricots, finely chopped
40g Forest Feast California Pistachios, shelled and chopped
A handful of chopped parsley
1 egg
Sea salt and crushed black pepper

Method:

- Make the stuffing by heating the olive oil in a non stick pan; fry the onion until very soft then remove from the heat and tip into a bowl.
- Add the chopped apricots and pistachios to the onion along with the breadcrumbs, chopped parsley, egg, salt, pepper and mix very well to bind the stuffing together.
- For each chicken fillet you need to lay 4 pieces of pancetta side by side on a chopping board to form a rectangular shape, now slice the chicken along the side, almost cutting the whole way through and open like a book. Place this onto the pancetta and fill with ¼ of the stuffing.
- Roll the chicken, pancetta and stuffing together - a bit like a Swiss roll.
- Repeat with the remaining ingredients, then place each stuffed and rolled fillet onto a non stick baking sheet and roast in a hot oven for around 25 minutes until the chicken is thoroughly cooked and the pancetta is crisp.
- Slice the chicken and arrange on plates to show the stuffing. Creamy mashed potato, green beans and maybe a little chicken gravy works a treat.

Easy home-made ice-cream, without a machine, combines our berries and Physalis. From the fantastic to the unbelievable they work together with the sugary creaminess and vanilla to make a sumptuous taste sensation. We're told the ice-cream will keep for about 2 weeks in your freezer, in a container with a lid, but we don't think it'll last that long.

Home-made Tutti Frutti Ice-cream

Serves 10

Ingredients:

Juice of 1 orange (about 100mls)
80g Forest Feast Fantastic Physalis
75g Forest Feast Sumptuous Strawberries
80g Forest Feast Bountiful Blackcurrants
70g Forest Feast Unbelievable Blueberries

For the cream:
750mls whipping cream
8 egg yolks
200g caster sugar
10 drops of vanilla extract

Method:

- Tip the physalis, strawberries, blackcurrants and blueberries into a saucepan and cover with orange juice. Bring to the boil for 2 - 3 minutes until most of the orange juice is absorbed, then remove from the heat and cool completely.
- Meanwhile, beat the egg yolks, sugar and vanilla extract together in a large bowl with an electric mixer until the mixture turns pale golden and doubles in volume, this will take about 7 minutes.
- Whip the cream to soft peaks and gently fold into the egg and sugar mixture.
- Tip into a large Tupperware container & pop it into the freezer.
- Allow the ice-cream to freeze for about 3 hours, then mix through the soaked fruit quickly and return to the freezer for at least 12 hours.
- It is important to allow 3 hours of freezing before mixing the fruit into the ice-cream, if you do not do this the fruit will sink to the bottom.
- For the best result remove it from the freezer and place in the fridge to soften a little before serving.

Pavlova is dead easy to make, we've added chopped hazelnuts for a nutty flavour and Perfect Pomegranate seeds that taste so delicious with cream, meringue and raspberries. We know we shouldn't.....but we will!

Pavlova with Hazelnuts, Raspberries and Pomegranate

An inspiring ingredient

Serves 6
Preheat oven to 150°C/300°F/gas mark 2.

Ingredients:

4 egg whites, at room temperature
300g caster sugar
1 heaped teaspoon of corn flour
1 teaspoon of vanilla extract

To decorate:
250mls whipping cream
50g Forest Feast Hazelnuts
1 large punnet of fresh raspberries
40g Forest Feast Perfect Pomegranate
A few sprigs of mint

Add chopped hazelnuts for a nutty flavour.

Method:

- Line a large baking tray (about 12 inch square) with baking parchment (do not use greaseproof paper as the Pavlovas will stick to it).
- Place the egg whites and sugar into a clean, grease free bowl and whisk with an electric mixer for about 10 minutes until thick, creamy and glossy. (If you turn the bowl upside down and the meringue doesn't move... it's perfect).
- Quickly whisk in the corn flour and vanilla extract.
- Either pipe or dollop six individual pavlovas onto your pre-prepared tray and place into a hot oven for 20 minutes, then turn the temperature off and allow the pavlovas to sit there until the oven cools completely. Don't open the oven door; as this will cause them to sink.
- Pour the hazelnuts into a sealable food bag, close the bag and bash with a rolling pin until the nuts resemble fine breadcrumbs.
- When the pavlovas are cold, use a palette knife to remove from the baking parchment and set onto plates ready to decorate with whipped cream, chopped hazelnuts, fresh raspberries, a sprinkling of Perfect Pomegranate and a few sprigs of mint.

Sprinkle with Perfect Pomegranate and mint

Sometimes there is no substitute for making a bit of a mess and none better than our Bountiful Blackberry Eton Mess. The combination of juicy, tart blackcurrants with silky smooth cream and softened lumps of sticky meringue make this an irresistible after dinner indulgence.

Blackcurrant Eton Mess

Serves 4

Ingredients:

80g Forest Feast Bountiful Blackcurrants
180mls red wine
Juice of 1 orange
4 drops of vanilla extract
56g of baked meringue
(we used 4 store bought small meringue nests)
250mls whipping cream
Fresh blackberries and mint to decorate

Method:

- Pour the red wine, orange juice and vanilla into a saucepan, add the blackcurrants and bring to the boil. Reduce the temperature to the lowest setting and simmer for about 5 minutes until the blackcurrants soften and the sauce thickens, remove from the heat and allow to cool completely.
- Whip the cream in a large mixing bowl, smash the meringue nests into little pieces and add along with the cold blackcurrants and sauce, mix well and spoon into glasses. Chill before decorating with fresh blackberries and fresh mint.

Makes 16 delicious blondies

We don't know if Blondies are more fun, but we do know they are a delicious twist on the much loved chocolate brownie. We have replaced the dark chocolate with white to enrich and contrast with the fruity sharpness of cranberries and the crunchy nutty pecans. Tastes good!

White Chocolate, Cranberry and Pecan Blondies

Makes 10 small squares
Preheat oven to 180°C/350°F/gas mark 4.
Grease and line a 20x23x4cm tin.

Ingredients:

200g chopped white chocolate
100g butter
100g soft light brown sugar
2 large eggs
110g plain flour
80g Forest Feast Incredible Cranberries
50g Forest Feast Pecans, chopped

Method:

- Place half of the white chocolate into a medium mixing bowl along with the butter.
- Half fill a medium saucepan with water and boil. When at boiling point, remove from the heat and set the mixing bowl on top to allow the butter and chocolate to gently melt.
- Using an electric mixer beat the eggs and sugar together in a large bowl until light and fluffy, then stir in the melted chocolate and butter, sift in the flour and stir gently.
- To finish the blondies add the cranberries, chopped pecans and remaining chopped white chocolate, then pour the mixture into the prepared tin.
- Bake in a hot oven for 30-35 minutes, to check if it is baked all the way through - lay your finger on top and press down gently - if it springs back up - it's ready.
- Allow to cool before eating.

Sumptuous Strawberries and cream work like a dream! We use our strawberries to turn a quick, basic cup cake into something spectacular. The strawberries almost melt in the oven and develop a sweet stickiness, a bit like jam, only better. A simple whirl of freshly whipped cream is enough to finish off these delicious little delights.

Strawberry and Cream Cup Cakes

Makes 12 cup cakes
Preheat oven to 180°C/350°F/gas mark 4.

Ingredients:

75g Forest Feast Sumptuous Strawberries
150g self-raising flour
120g caster sugar
150g butter
3 medium eggs

To decorate:
250mls whipped cream
6 fresh strawberries

Method:

- Finely chop the dried strawberries and set aside while you make the cake mixture.
- Sift the flour and place in a bowl along with the sugar, softened butter and eggs. Beat together with an electric mixer until the mixture is smooth and slightly lighter in colour.
- Fold the chopped strawberries into the cake batter.
- Line the cup cake tin with paper cup cake cases and three quarter fill each case with the strawberry batter.
- Bake the cakes for 18-20 minutes. You can tell they are done when they have risen up, are golden in colour, and spring back into shape when lightly pressed.
- Remove from the oven and cool completely.
- To decorate: Pipe a swirl of cream on top and decorate with fresh strawberries.

Pina-colada Cup Cakes

Pineapple and coconut go well together as another option for cup cakes, but it's important to give our Pineapple Rings a good soaking before use and then chop them up as finely as you can.

Makes 12 cup cakes
Preheat oven to 180°C/350°F/gas mark 4.

Ingredients: – as above

Replace Strawberries with:
75g Forest Feast Pineapple Rings, (must be soaked in warm water for 10 minutes, dried & very finely chopped)
30g desiccated coconut

For the cream:
125g mascarpone cheese
15g caster sugar
25g desiccated coconut
100mls whipping cream, whipped
To decorate: White chocolate shavings

Method:

- Follow method as above, adding the pineapple and coconut in place of the strawberries.
- To make the cream: Place the mascarpone, sugar, coconut and whipping cream into a large mixing bowl and whisk vigorously by hand for a minute until you have a softly whipped cream.
- To decorate, pipe a swirl of the coconut cream on top and decorate with white chocolate shavings.

The Hard Rock of tray bakes combines our Scrumptious Sour Cherries and Luxury Mixed Nut & Raisin with a mass of melted chocolate for the ultimate chocolate fix. Let's hit that Rocky Road.

Fantastic Rocky Roads

Makes 18
9 inch square tin, lined with baking parchment

Ingredients:

150g butter
300g good quality milk chocolate
150g golden syrup (roughly 3 tablespoons)
200g digestive biscuits, roughly broken
100g mini marshmallows
75g Forest Feast Luxury Mixed Nut & Raisin
80g Forest Feast Scrumptious Sour Cherries

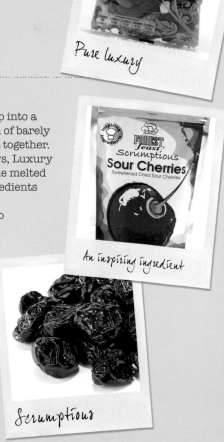

Pure luxury

An inspiring ingredient

Scrumptious

Method:

- Place the butter, chocolate and golden syrup into a heatproof mixing bowl and place over a pan of barely simmering water, allow them to gently melt together.
- Add the broken biscuits, mini marshmallows, Luxury Mixed Nut & Raisin and Sour Cherries to the melted mixture. Stir well to ensure all the dry ingredients are coated in the chocolate mixture.
- Pour into the prepared tin and chill for up to 4 hours until completely cold and set. Cut into 18 small squares.
- They can be stored in an airtight container for up to 1 week.

Fudge with the exotic flavours of mango, pineapple and pomegranate. It's looking good and tasting even better.

Exotic Fruit Fudge

Makes 36 pieces

You will need:

a sugar thermometer, electric hand mixer and a
15cm (6 inch) square tin, lightly buttered and lined with greaseproof paper.

Ingredients:

130g Forest Feast Exotic Dried Mango
125g Forest Feast Tropical Dried Pineapple Rings
80g Forest Feast Perfect Pomegranate
450g granulated sugar
1 tin of condensed milk (397g)
50g unsalted butter
125mls water

Method:

- Chop the mango and pineapple as finely as you possibly can with a large sharp knife, mix in the pomegranate and set aside.
- To make the fudge, put the sugar, condensed milk, butter and water into a heavy-based saucepan and stir over a gentle heat until the sugar has completely dissolved.
- Turn the heat up full and cook for about 15 minutes until the temperature registers 116°C on the sugar thermometer (soft ball stage, ensuring that the fudge will set). Stir well as the sugar will catch at the bottom of the pan, but don't worry, these caramelized bits will mix into the fudge and be delicious. Keep stirring continuously as you cook for a further 5 minutes until golden.
- Pour the liquid fudge into a clean mixing bowl along with the prepared dried fruit and beat with an electric mixer for 2 minutes, this will thicken the mixture and allow it to develop a fudge texture. Pour into the prepared tin, allowing the fudge to cool and set completely before cutting into bite size pieces and storing in an airtight container.

Party nuts

You'll probably think we're nuts but some of our firm favourites like to get spruced up when they hear we're having a party.

Salt and Chilli Almonds

Ingredients:
Olive oil
250g Forest Feast Almonds
A handful of sea salt
Mild chilli powder

Method:
- Pour a good glug of olive oil onto a roasting tray and add 250g of Forest Feast Almonds.
- Place into a hot oven for about 20 minutes and then drain the nuts on a piece of kitchen roll.
- Quickly sprinkle with sea salt and ground mild chilli powder, mix well until evenly coated and serve.
- The almonds are best eaten immediately but you can store them in an airtight container for 3 - 4 days.

Oven roasted

Hot Chilli Nuts

Simply heat a large wok or frying pan to a medium heat and add the Forest Feast Chilli Nuts. Stir for about 5 minutes until they have warmed through - delicious!

Delicious warmed through

Spiced Party Nuts

Ingredients:
400g Forest Feast Natural Mixed Nuts
40g butter
1 tablespoon of olive oil
1 tablespoon of Worcestershire sauce
¼ teaspoon of garlic powder
1 teaspoon of paprika
½ teaspoon of cayenne pepper

Method:
- Melt the butter with the olive oil.
- Add the Worcestershire sauce, garlic powder, paprika and cayenne pepper and mix well.
- Mix approximately 400g of Forest Feast Natural Mixed Nuts with the spiced oil and roast in the oven for around 40 minutes at 150°C.

Mix with spiced oil and roast for 40 minutes

Devils Bite Dip

For a really good dip simply empty a packet of Forest Feast Devils Bite into a food processor and whiz until you have a spicy crumble. Warm some crispy bread in a hot oven and tear into chunks, then dip firstly into a little virgin olive oil and then into the spicy powder.

Give your dip some bite

These little devils are so easy to make– prepare them in advance and keep in the fridge until you're ready to cook, giving you plenty of time to slip on your dancing shoes. The sweet fruit cuts through the salty pancetta and will really get your party started!

Medjool Devils on Horseback

Makes 24
Preheat oven to 160°C/325°F/ Gas Mark 3

Ingredients:

24 Forest Feast Medjool Dates
12 Forest Feast Malatya Apricots
12 rashers of pancetta

Method:

- Make an incision in the Medjool dates, removing the stone.
- Slice the Malatya apricots in half, stuffing all the dates with a piece of apricot.
- Cut the pancetta rashers in half and place a stuffed date in the centre of each, roll up tightly securing with a cocktail stick.
- Set on a baking tray and bake at 160°C for 10 minutes until the dates are soft and pancetta is crispy.

...giving you time to look fabulous

Medjool
Dates

authentic dried fruit

180g ℮

Our Tropical Dried Pineapple brings a taste of the exotics with this cool yoghurt dip - Enjoy after a summer's barbeque in the garden and imagine you're in the Tropics.

Pineapple Chips and Dip

Serves 4

Ingredients:

125mls natural low fat yoghurt
A good pinch of chopped fresh chilli
1 tablespoon of mint leaves, chopped
A squeeze of lemon juice

To serve:

Forest Feast Tropical Dried Pineapple Rings, cut into quarters.

Method:

- Place the yoghurt into a bowl, add the chilli, mint leaves and a squeeze of lemon juice. Mix well and serve with quarters of Forest Feast Tropical Dried Pineapple Rings for dipping.

OPEN • STAY FRESH • RESEALABLE

FOREST
feast

Tropical Dried

Pineappl

Rings

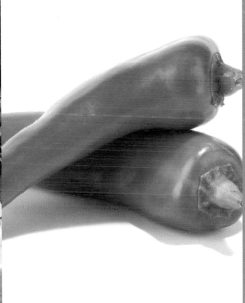

Powerhouse Cavendish Banana covered in rich dark chocolate makes the perfect 'pick me up'. Give to someone as a hand-made gift, just wrap in tissue paper and put in a pretty box.

Cavendish Banana Chocos

Makes about 32

Ingredients:

200g dark chocolate (minimum 50% cocoa)
200g Forest Feast Cavendish Banana

To Decorate:

A little white chocolate.

Method:

- Gently melt the dark chocolate in a large mixing bowl.
- Quickly add Forest Feast Cavendish Banana and coat each piece well.
- Carefully remove each piece of banana from the chocolate with a fork and allow to dry on baking parchment.
- Melt a little white chocolate and drizzle over each Banana Choco for decoration.

Rich dark chocolate makes the perfect 'pick me up'

Berries & Cherries in Red Wine

Serves 4

Ingredients:

180mls red wine
170g Forest Feast Berries & Cherries
2 tablespoons of caster sugar
4 drops of vanilla extract
Juice of 1 large orange
Juice of ½ a lemon

Simply delicious

Method:

- Pour the red wine into a saucepan with the caster sugar, vanilla extract and the orange and lemon juice.
- Boil for 5 minutes then reduce temperature, add Forest Feast Berries & Cherries and simmer for 10 minutes.
- Remove from heat and rest for 15 minutes then serve warm in glasses with a scoop of good quality vanilla ice-cream.

Poached Malatya Apricots

Serves 4

Ingredients:

250mls orange juice
30g honey
A small handful of chopped mint
130g Forest Feast Malatya Apricots

Method:

- Pour the orange juice into a medium sized saucepan along with the honey and chopped mint.
- Bring to the boil, reduce the heat to the lowest setting and simmer for 7 or 8 minutes until it starts to thicken.
- Add the Forest Feast Malatya Apricots and simmer for another 10 minutes. Sprinkle on some chopped fresh mint and serve warm with vanilla ice-cream.

Serve with vanilla ice-cream

Boozy Christmas Pudding

Makes 2 x 1.25kg/3lb moulds

Ingredients:

250g Forest Feast Raisins
350g Forest Feast Sultanas
125g Forest Feast Berries & Cherries
125g Forest Feast Medjool Dates,
finely chopped
100g Forest Feast Cut Mixed Peel
125g Forest Feast Malatya Apricots,
finely chopped
80g Forest Feast Gorgeous Goji berries
(optional)
80g Forest Feast Incredible
Cranberries
The juice & finely grated rind of 1 lemon
The juice & finely grated rind of 1 orange

425mls Guinness
450g unsalted butter,
at room temperature
450g light muscovado sugar
6 eggs
125g plain flour
1 teaspoon of ground nutmeg
2 teaspoon of ground mixed spice
1 teaspoon of ground cinnamon
1 teaspoon of ground cloves
1 teaspoon of baking powder
1 teaspoon of salt
450g fresh white breadcrumbs
1 large Bramley apple, peeled, cored
and grated (approximately 225g)

Method to prepare the fruit :

- Place the raisins, sultanas, Berries & Cherries, dates, mixed peel, apricots, goji berries and cranberries in a large bowl with the fruit juice and rind. Pour in the Guinness, stirring until well combined. Cover with cling film and set aside to soak, for at least 24 hours, as fruit needs to totally absorb the Guinness - you should stir occasionally.

To make the pudding:

- Use an electric mixer to cream the butter and sugar in a large bowl until light and fluffy. Gradually add the eggs, mixing well after each addition and add a handful of flour to prevent curdling.
- Sift the flour, spices and salt together and fold, along with the breadcrumbs into the butter mixture.
- Add the grated apple and finally stir in the soaked dried fruit with any remaining liquid.
- Divide the mixture into 2 x 1.25kg/3lb moulds, cover with cling film or greaseproof paper and tie with string. In the bottom of a large saucepan, place a large cookie cutter, setting a small plate on top and then set the pudding on the plate. Fill to just below the plate with water (Do not allow the bottom of the pudding moulds to sit directly on the base of the pan; they need to be raised up at least 2–3cm). Cover with foil and steam for 3-4 hours until cooked through. Be sure to watch the pan to ensure that it doesn't boil dry and keep the water at a constant gentle boil.
- After steaming leave to cool completely, then store in a cool, dark place for up to 1 year.
- On Christmas day, steam the pudding for about 1½ hours until heated through.

Inspiring Ingredients

By Kestrel Foods Ltd.

Published by:
Kestrel Foods Ltd.
Unit 8 Carn Drive, Carn Industrial Estate,
Portadown
Co.Armagh
BT63 5WJ

The team at Forest Feast are fanatical about dried fruit and nuts but with so many other ingredients to consider, for our recipe book, we thought we'd better call in an expert. Karyn Booth, food stylist and chef, is a local girl with loads of knowledge having worked in the Ritz Hotel London, in the house of Albert Roux and in Sir Terence Conran's Sartoria on Saville Road. We think Karyn has loads of great ideas for Forest Feast – we hope you like them too.

Printed and bound in Hong Kong by Great Wall Printing Company Limited.
A catalogue record for this book is available from the British Library

ISBN 978-0-9565885-0-0